# Ain't Life a Beach?

Life is an ongoing challenge that changes from moment to moment—it can bring in or release things that can either nourish or devastate you. How you respond to those times will determine your success in life.

*Dr. Linda Andrade Wheeler*

My gratitude is extended to those who continually share their
stories with me, some of which are included in this book. They
have brought "realness" and warmth to this book.

Reviewed and edited by:
Milt Wheeler
Milton & Noi Wheeler
Garrett Wheeler
Lance & Kimberly Wheeler

Book Design by Joe Hunt
Photography by Veronica Carmona


Published and distributed by:

ISLAND HERITAGE
P U B L I S H I N G
94-411 KŌ'AKI STREET
WAIPAHU, HAWAI'I 96797

Orders: (800) 468-2800
Information: (808) 564-8800
Fax (808) 564-8877
**islandheritage.com**

ISBN 0-89610-519-9
First Edition, First Printing 2003

Printed in Hong Kong

# Contents

To my sisters,

Marie Achi, Janice Donohoo,
Stacey Eaton and Karen Stovall

You made the journey
from little girls to grown
women fantastic!
You are not only
my dear sisters,
but my best friends as well.
Life's changes have made
you even more beautiful
with the passing of time.

# Introduction

This is a book on the power of changes (ideas), choices (directions) and challenges (risks). It will give you a unique perspective for viewing change, making choices that enhance and enrich your life, and help you to face the challenges that life may present to you. What you will get out of this book is entirely dependent upon what you put into it. Remember, when you swim in shallow water, you will gather only what is washed close to shore. However, it is in the deeper recesses of your mind that your dive will bring up more valuable and long-lasting lessons. It definitely will help you to probe into your own life and ask very important questions, like: Who am I? What do I value in life? What makes me happy? How do I handle the changes in my life? Do I make thoughtful and responsible choices? How do I want to be remembered? and more.

The beach serves as a wonderful metaphor in that the journey of life is one of constant rhythm, yet open to unpredictable events. Anyone can handle the steady pace of routine and flow with the tide, but it takes extraordinary people to effectively manage life's tsunamis—situations, events, people, etc. that can either wipe out all that you've accomplished or crush your dreams. It is in those challenging times that you are faced with the choice to go on or give up. What you choose to do in handling those difficult times can propel you to greatness or sink you to your lowest emotional depths.

Life is a continual process of letting go and moving forward, letting go and moving forward. You cannot keep everything you want in life—no matter how much you want it. You might lose that which you really do not want to lose; then there are things you might want to release to make life more manageable for yourself. It is then that you must dive to the depths of your soul—for the things at the deepest levels of the ocean are far more precious, more valued because of the challenge of getting to them. It is so with your inner-most thoughts and feelings, which dwell in the deepest part of your soul.

There are times when your soul is set on fire and deeply cherished dreams must die—like the fragile sand castles that you built on the beach. And you are forced once again to create new visions and weave new tapestries from the fragments of the old. Yet these new visions, born from the fire of wisdom at the deepest level of your soul, may well become far more powerful, more expansive, than what once was, and so you weave and mend, rearranging the pieces of your life into patterns that reflect your newly won strength gained through struggle. You will survive, go on, and ultimately thrive, not because of the immense challenges you will face in life, but truly by how you meet and live through them. It is this ebb and flow of life that will be exciting as you learn to live with the unpredictable—the surprises of experiencing life on a day-to-day basis. You can control what life brings to you and what you release to it. It is the changes, choices and challenges that you face in life that will bring you the greatest rewards.

Many a beach has been destroyed by unpredictable or unexpected elements that have altered its unique configuration. What once was can never be the same again. You must learn to accept the changes in life, and alterations in yourself and others that were unforeseen, because all of us must change to some degree to find the very best in ourselves. Do not seek perfection, for it will torment you; rather, focus on continuous improvement—it will delight and astonish you.

**B**e yourself despite the changes that can interrupt your life so drastically that you think you will never be the same again. It is then that you must believe that although things may not take on as much meaning as before, you will bring meaning back to life.

**E**xamine the promises and opportunities that roll in and out of your life—know which ones to catch and which ones to let go. They can change your life.

**A**cknowledge, accept, appreciate and act upon that which you want to change. That change can cause a ripple that may have long-lasting effects in your life.

**C**reate better ways and new things by thinking and acting differently. You bring "spirit" to places, things and people when you bring the best of yourself—and then act in sync with them.

**H**ave a broad perspective of life that encompasses everything in the universe. You will begin to realize the value of life and your role in it.

B e yourself despite the changes that can interrupt your life so drastically that you think you will never be the same again. It is then that you must believe that although things may not take on as much meaning as before, you will bring meaning back to life.

Nothing ever stays the same. There is really no forever. Everything comes to an end. Everything has a beginning. An end only signals a new beginning. Beginnings will always have ends. The cycle of life is constant in its changes. Changes are the only constant thing you can expect of life.

How you respond to the continual changes in your life will teach you more about yourself than anything else. In learning how to manage your life despite the changes that will occur, you come to understand who you are and what it means to be a human being. If you expect to find happiness in this life, you must certainly know who you are and value who you are.

My daughter-in-law Kim e-mailed me a wonderful story that serves as a great reminder. A well-known speaker started off his seminar by holding up a twenty-dollar bill. He asked the room of two hundred, "Who in here would like the twenty-dollar bill?" Hands started going up throughout the room and the speaker said, "I'm going to give this twenty-dollar bill away, but first, watch this."

The speaker then crumpled up the twenty-dollar bill tightly and asked if anyone still wanted it. Again, hands went up. "Well," he continued, "what if I do this?" and the speaker dropped the crumpled twenty-dollar bill on the floor and ground it underfoot. "Anyone still want it?" Again, many hands went up, although some were becoming skeptical. "You all have learned a valuable lesson here: no matter what I did to this money, you still wanted it because it did not decrease in value. It is still worth twenty dollars, no matter if it is ragged and worn."

Many times in our lives we are dropped, crumpled and ground into the dirt by the decisions we make and the circumstances that come our way. We feel that we are worthless. But no matter what has happened or what will happen, we will never lose our value— dirty or clean, crumpled or carefully creased—we are still priceless to those who love us.

Unlike the twenty-dollar bill, we often increase in value because of life's struggles and challenges. The worth of our lives comes not in what we do or who we know, but in who we are. We are all very special, believe it.

At this point, it is time to look inside yourself. What do you believe about yourself? What do you think about the people around you? How is your philosophy of life opening up new doors in your life, or closing them—doors that were once open to you?

You need to remember that your own emotions will test what kind of human being you are. Sometimes even feelings of hurt, rejection and sadness can help to keep you human and humble. It is when you forget these feelings that you become callous and arrogant. You can make yourself invisible to the negative things you caused in your life. But that's the easy way out—the coward's approach to avoiding the pain and suffering. You must face your fears if you want to conquer them.

Things don't change people, people change things. You are powerful in creating the life you want. Your faith in yourself and what you can do will give you the personal power to conquer adversity. Success will follow.

Believe in yourself and what it is that you can do. The magic of belief is far greater than most realize. The greatest weakness that human beings have is the lack of belief in themselves—knowing how powerful they are. Your chances for success in any undertaking can always be measured by your belief in yourself. You will get from life what you think you richly deserve.

Make a conscious effort to change what is not working in your life. You cannot change the past, what people will do, and the inevitable. What you can change, however, is how you manage yourself.

## It Matters Not!

The smile on your face is worth much more than the designer label on your outfit. You build your own worth as a person. No one can make you into a valuable person; you do this all on your own. Others can support that worth, but you build, maintain and sustain the value of you.

In our neighborhood, we had a well-respected and prominent businessman, Mr. Milligan, who was the father of two girls and one boy. He wanted his children to have the sense that their self-worth was measured by the things they did for others, not by the wealth that they possessed. He wanted them to know that money was not the most important factor in measuring the worth of a person.

To do this, he told his family that each month they would all go out to dine if they could first go to a thrift shop and buy all that they needed there to attire themselves for the evening. If they could do that, he was willing to treat them to the finest restaurants in town. Every family member was given ten dollars to get his or her complete outfit.

Eventually, they became great shoppers at the thrift shop—seeking out the clothes that matched their personalities and tastes (which were all so different). Their dad marveled at their creativity and sense of fun in doing that. When they entered the fine restaurants, they all seemed appropriately dressed and no one noticed what labels they wore. No one knew and no one cared. They looked good, felt good, and had a lot of fun. For years, this was Mr. Milligan's usual monthly family activity until his children left home for mainland colleges.

Mr. Milligan was very proud of himself when his eldest daughter, who had made her millions in investments, became the first female governor of the Rotary Club (the largest service club in the world) in her state. His youngest daughter, who was married to one of the most well-respected ministers in the country, became a newspaper columnist on family matters, encouraging parents to help children to see the power within themselves and their important role in developing values to promote goodness. And his only son became a physician and the father of five children, all of whom look forward to their grandfather's periodic visits when they can all go shopping—yes, at thrift shops, and then dining—at the best restaurants in town.

Never underestimate your power to influence a person. You are very important in influencing people—whether you intend to or not—just by being the person you are.

You have a chance to change the way people look at life, to enlarge the experiences of others, and to communicate with others through expressing your own unique perspective.

You have such power in influencing people around you—by your level of personal excellence. In fact, many people attribute some degree of their happiness to others who have helped them or made their lives easier in some way. A Japanese saying, *Okage sama de,* which means, "I am who I am because of you," says it best. You can either bring light or darkness to other people's lives. You get to choose. You can encourage them to look for the best in life, or focus on the negative aspects of it. How you think and eventually how you behave tell people what you value the most in life. If people are important to you, you will be considerate, patient and caring in your interactions with them.

I once heard a seminar leader speak of setting priorities. She was telling the audience how they could examine their priorities and then change those priorities at will by dropping the things that were of least importance to them, and focusing on the ones that mattered the most at the time of their examination. She said that making the necessary changes in one's life was like creating the right size of kukui nut lei to wear. Some liked their leis short; some longer—it all depended upon the individual's preference and loading capacity. She said that if your lei was too long, you could shorten it by eliminating kukui nuts from the lei. The discarded kukui nuts could represent people, things or situations that were cluttering your life. By going through this examination and elimination process, you could shorten your list of priorities and focus on the most important things in your life.

While I could see the dropping of inanimate things and situations—such as releasing yourself from the maintenance of expensive houses, cars and clothes, and from group associations that can sap your energy and take time away from your priorities in life, it bothered me how one could suggest to other people that they drop people from their lives as if they were kukui nuts. Something was wrong in this analogy. How do you preserve the human dignity of a person while attempting to drop that person from your life? It seems to me that life rewards you with lasting friends when you nurture caring relationships that honor the ebb and flow of life. And should the time for good-byes occur, remember the old adage, "All is well that ends well." You must be careful to separate in good spirits, rather than to split the friendship with a sharp knife that cuts into the spirit of caring.

There are certain periods of your life when you will make decisions that do not include certain people in your life. However, don't discard them as if they were inanimate things—kukui nuts that have no heart, no feelings. Human beings do have hearts; they do feel the rejection, loss and trauma of not being valued by someone any longer. It is a time to be careful about bruising people's hearts. The caring person will remember how much the individual was valued and the memories attached to that. This process will help you to soften the separation, and the new placement of that person. How cruel not to do this kind act—to truly recognize someone is to show kindness to that person. Everyone can make the conscious choice to be kind to people. That is a choice you make yourself. After all, once you touch a person's heart with kindness, you leave a lasting imprint no one else can erase.

You choose what strategy you will use to set your new priorities. In this decision-making process, you can either demonstrate what a terrific person you are, or lose your own self-worth as a responsible human being. If you no longer are viewed as a compassionate and caring person, you set yourself up for others to treat you that way. If you don't care, why should anyone care about you? Once you hurt someone badly, what keeps you from hurting the next person in your life? You set the patterns in your life. So if you have that enormous power to create the kind of life you want, wouldn't you want to navigate your life to work for you, not against you?

≈≈≈

# Grains of Sand

## (A Dozen Quotes)

≈≈≈

Who you are makes a difference.

≈≈≈

The greatest compliment
anyone can give another is to
expect the very best of that person.

≈≈≈

Never let your successes go to your head.
Never let your failures get to your heart.

≈≈≈

Believe in what you do and do it well.

≈≈≈

≈≈≈

Know who you are at all times.
Anchor yourself securely, but set your
sails for continuous self-discovery
and self-renewal.

≈≈≈

Change of position changes meaning.
However, know when and how to change.
Changing seats on the *Titanic* would not
have made a difference.

≈≈≈

You teach who you are.

≈≈≈

Self-criticism and negative thinking are
learned and can be unlearned.

≈≈≈

≈≈≈

When you face your problems is when you
will find the opportunities for growth.

≈≈≈

If you don't like something, change it.
If you can't change it,
change the way you look at it.

≈≈≈

It is a funny thing about life:
if you refuse to accept anything but the best,
you very often get it.

≈≈≈

If you don't like how you are going
to be remembered, it is not too
late to change.

≈≈≈

xamine the promises and opportunities that roll in and out of your life—know which ones to catch and which ones to let go. They can change your life.

The minute you realize the importance that changes play in your life, you will begin to prioritize what it is you would like from life. It is a matter of choice—a process of discernment—what to keep, what to let go. It is really up to you. You have the power to do that; you alone will reap the rewards or suffer the consequences. That is the nature of choices. Whether you make a good or bad choice, there is always a consequence. It is in that realization of what is most important to you that you acquire the discipline to focus your energy on the things and people you have chosen to give your time and attention to, so that you will grow and be nourished. By doing this, you will not only survive, but thrive, because your energies and efforts will be focused on that which matters most in your life.

Change is a very personal matter. Everyone will experience changes in his or her lifetime. The challenge for each person facing change is the rare opportunity to test the flexibility, adaptability and resiliency not only to survive the changes, but to flourish personally and professionally from them.

The journey of life is not a static one—it is a dynamic path with many currents, channeled in the choices that you make for yourself. No one is exempt from this decision-making process. You are continually evolving. Your consistent rhythm is permanent, and everything else is temporary. It is your life's song, the one you play for yourself.

You make choices on an everyday basis. Some choices you hold onto dearly because they work for you, and others you let go to make yourself a better person. Like the waves that wash the shore of stuff I left behind, the choices you release can bring new and better opportunities to enrich your life. The wonder is that you can create new choices each day, as the ocean of life washes away your previously worn choices.

That is the nature of life—ever changing, and ever challenging. Like on great beaches everywhere, the ocean will bring to shore treasures as well as meaningless objects. Sometimes the people who you left behind can come back into your life, like driftwood on the shore. You need to learn to discern who and what will nourish you or destroy you, just as you must discern what you release to the world that either hurts or helps you. It is in this context of learning that you begin to discern what in the world is worthy of your time and attention. You only get from life what you are willing to put into it.

Every day you are asked to make choices: what clothes to wear, what you will have for breakfast, what attitude you will choose for the day, how you will behave to those around you, what activities you will engage in, how much money you will spend, which person(s) you will spend your time with that day, and so on. And many times, you make those choices unconsciously without really considering which choice will be the best one for you, or what you expect to gain through that particular decision.

You operate on so many levels when making decisions for yourself. You make choices according to your own beliefs about yourself and what you believe your purpose is here on earth. You may sometimes make choices to impress others—expensive clothes, cars, houses, exclusive friends, club memberships. At other times, you may want to gain self-satisfaction in life and your choices are clear and apparent: material things are not the most important things in your life—your focus is on people and how you can make a difference in their lives. You get to choose how you want to live, and what priorities you set for yourself. In light of this great power of choice, be cognizant of why you make your choices. That realization will help you get the results you hoped for and the consequences you expected. That is how you manage and control your own life.

As I sit here today writing, it is my father's birthday. He was born on November 11, 1911. Yes, 11/11/11. My father was very proud of those numbers and felt honored to have been born on Veteran's Day.

But my father was special not only for his distinctive birthdate, but for the person he was. He was a private man, who enjoyed the peace of silence and the stimulation of intellectual conversation. He was well read on a variety of subjects, wrote in an elegant script, expressed his honest opinion even when other people's views differed, and honored his religious beliefs.

In his daily life, he was a man of rhythm and pattern, predictable as the ebb and flow of the tide. Yet he was flexible and bendable like the changing surf whenever he felt it necessary.

Although my father was proud of being a celebrated sportsman in his youth, his greatest triumphs and challenges came as a husband to an exciting and community-minded wife, and father to his five daughters, whom he referred to as "the jewels on my crown." We were all special to him, and each of us knew that.

After my father's funeral, my sisters and I sat around the dinner table reminiscing about our father and the experiences we each had with him. Throughout his seventy-eight years, he was a pillar of strength. He was always there for us when we needed him—to give us that special wink or warm, handsome smile, gentle pat on the head, or comforting hug, and in the way he took interest in what we had to share with him.

At one point I told my sisters how special I felt every time Daddy would call to me and take me out to the front steps to sit with him. We would go out to the front porch where we watched the cars passing by under the huge monkeypod trees that formed an arch over the two-way main street that passed by our home.

He would always sit at the top of the steps leading to the porch. Automatically I would position myself between his legs on the lower step and place my arms on his legs. Instinctively he would look at my hands and inspect my nails. My father always liked to keep his nails short and clean. Somehow, as a young girl, I always felt that this ritual with me was to get me to do that as well, because he would always get his nail clippers out and start trimming and grooming my nails.

Well, before I ended my story, each of my other sisters chimed in, "Daddy did that with me too!" And each of them told her story of her "nail grooming" session with Daddy. What I thought was an exclusive session with me turned out to be our father's effective way of getting to talk to his five daughters privately.

However, I realized it wasn't the grooming of our nails that was important to my father; it was how he got to know what was happening in our lives at the time. Daddy had a high degree of integrity and commitment to those he loved. He made us feel secure, understood and important by listening to us intently and asking pertinent questions. Worries seemed to dissipate after a discussion with Daddy. He always ended his counsel with the expression, "No scare um." Daddy never told us explicitly what to do. He always made us look at our own problems and search within ourselves to find the best solution. He taught us that the reality of a situation is sometimes different from our perception of it.

It was amazing to me how the few questions my father asked me prompted responses that had me thinking and sharing, and sometimes crying or laughing. It was either a good cleansing or a healing session whenever I spent those moments with the man I loved so much in life. My father's kindness and gentle ways helped to shape the person I envisioned for myself.

What my father read, what he ate, who he saw, where he went, and the gifts that he gave were always carefully thought out. Each had its purpose and meaning for Dad. He designed his life to fully acknowledge and appreciate those he loved. It seemed that my father had a special mission in life—

to give his daughters a realistic version of what a loving, committed and responsible family man looks like in everyday life.

Today, when I visit his grave site and see the digits of his birthdate and the date he died clearly separated by a dash in between, I know that the dash—symbolic of the life he lived—was what really made my father special.

Dad left us with such fond memories, interwoven with wonderful and lasting experiences of a happy childhood and colorful island expressions, such as, "Smile, no worry—not going help" (whenever we were going through tough times); "I'll tune you up" (whenever we were sad or naughty); "I'm making my rounds" (when he was out and we couldn't reach him); "I'm busy doing grandpa things" (when he was doing something for our kids); "What's the matter—if can, can...if cannot, cannot" (whenever we felt guilty for not being able to do something for some-one); and many other unique expressions that con-veyed profound wisdom.

On one of our family gatherings, my sisters and I were at dinner having a wonderful time talking about how we were beginning to forget things—periodic lapses of memory—when one of my younger sisters, Jan, asked if we remembered Mr. Yuri, a longtime Maui restaurateur.

She said that she marveled at this eighty-four-year-old gentleman's sustaining ability to remember people who dined at his restaurant. One of the things he loved doing was to take pictures of his customers, and then place them on the walls and ceiling, which were covered with these pictures. Every time repeat customers entered his restaurant, Mr. Yuri would take them over to a specific section of the dining area, and show them their picture. He never skipped a beat—he always matched the person with the picture. He really was terrific in associating faces and names.

One day Jan was at the local shopping center when she suddenly came upon Mr. Yuri looking very puzzled and disoriented. He smiled and said hi to her. She stopped to talk to him and asked if she could help him with anything. He looked at her very sheepishly and said, "I am afraid that I have forgotten where I parked. I cannot find my car." Of course she helped him until he did find his car; but she couldn't get over the fact that this man who loved people, who never forgot their faces, could not remember where he had parked his car.

Somehow Jan sensed that his priority wasn't really remembering inanimate things—it was really people he wished to remember. In your own life, you get to choose your own priorities: some things are simply not as important as others.

≈≈≈

# Grains of Sand

(A Dozen Quotes)

≈≈≈

You cannot help people permanently
by helping them do things that they
should or could do for themselves.

≈≈≈

We get back what we give out.

≈≈≈

Instead of trying to hang
onto the past, grab hold of the future.

≈≈≈

You are who you are by the
choices you make.

≈≈≈

≈≈≈

You either dream it, feel it, or live it—
what you do determines your happiness.

≈≈≈

You can either ride the waves or
be pounded by them—it's up to you.

≈≈≈

You choose what you are going to face
and how you are going to face it.

≈≈≈

Everything in life is a matter of give and
take—you control what goes out of your life
and what comes back into your life.

≈≈≈

≈≈≈

What you are creates who you are.
You are, in the most literal sense, exactly
what you believe you are. You get what
you think you deserve.

≈≈≈

A beach is a beach only to those who
do not know the ocean. To those familiar with
the sea, the beach is the storyteller
of its surroundings.

≈≈≈

Everyone has the chance to make a
difference in someone else's life.

≈≈≈

Give people more than they expect,
and do it cheerfully.

≈≈≈

cknowledge, accept, appreciate and act upon that which you want to change. That change can cause a ripple that may have long-lasting effects in your life.

You have to accept life's mysteries and realities to experience its joys. To have harmony and peace of mind, use common sense and good judgment in dealing with adversities. It is through the consistency and clarity with which you say and do things that others will understand and know who you are.

If you haven't already noticed it, you have great power in placing value on things, people and situations. That's why, for example, when you see someone who is attractive and very much in love with someone who is not at all attractive, it makes you wonder. But on the other hand, if you say, "It matters not... " about observable things, and go for what's inside of people...your values are at work. A situation holds no more power than you give it. It is when you value something, that you give meaning to it.

It is sometimes in our most challenging moments that we find great opportunity to become better human beings. How we manage ourselves makes all the difference in creating opportunity out of crisis. There are two kinds of people in the world—those who make commitments and those who keep them. Commitment is an attitude.

When you make a promise, do everything in your power to keep it. Your commitment is measured by how you keep your word to others. You can choose to be a pillar of strength, or weak in terms of commitment. The choice is yours. The following story illustrates the tremendous impact a father's commitment can have on his family.

# A Father's Gift to His Family

On one of my off-island instructional trips, I had the good fortune of meeting a person who was to give me a fresh perspective on what it means to be a father. He was the representative of the company whose employees I was training that day. He had been assigned the task of transporting me from the airport to our training site.

As air transportation to Moloka'i was limited, I was forced to schedule myself on the earliest flight, which was approximately an hour and a half before the seminar began. On my arrival, I saw him waiting patiently against a State of Hawai'i vehicle, looking directly at me, as if he already knew who I was. We had never met before, but it seemed like an old friend was giving me a ride to where I needed to go.

That is how I met Pete Arceo, a forty-two-year-old man, whose openness gave me a peek into his private world.

Along the way to the company headquarters, we talked of his roots on his home island and about his family. I casually mentioned that one of the most peaceful scenes in my mind was the Moloka'i Hotel's restaurant lānai, bordered by the calm morning sea. I had conducted a session for teachers there the year before, and still remembered the serenity of the place with fondness.

Upon arriving at the company facility, the administrator of the regional office was deeply involved in completing a task before the training. He informed us that the participants would start arriving at the site in about an hour, and asked Pete if he would take me for a cup of coffee. Having rushed that morning to catch the early flight, I readily accepted. Pete obliged and off we went down the road until we arrived at the Moloka'i Hotel restaurant.

It impressed me that Pete recalled how I had said I enjoyed the view from the restaurant's lānai, and how he was giving me another opportunity to enjoy that kind of tranquillity. When we arrived, Pete's friend offered us some complimentary coffee, and we sat at a table near the edge of the ocean.

What transpired after that surprised and delighted me. Pete began to tell me his life's story, as if I were a friend he had known for many years. I welcomed the trust he gave me to know more about where he came from, the struggles he had endured as a young person, what he wanted to change in his life, and how he was making that happen.

In the peace of this Hawaiian tranquillity, Pete began to tell me his story of growing up on Moloka'i and the hard life he experienced as a young boy. Pete shared how he and his older brother were tossed from household to household after his parents' divorce. The boys were just seven and nine years old, but they understood fully that there was nowhere that they felt safe or loved. They were never in one place long enough to establish any meaningful relationships with either of their parents, or the relatives who helped care for them for short periods.

Their home life was gloomy and devoid of love. Pete's father struggled to make a living. He lived with his two sons in a converted cargo container with makeshift beds of beer cases stacked three boxes tall. It was the only kind of bed Pete and his brother ever slept on at his father's place.

Pete's paternal aunts, who lived next door in a house, helped to raise Pete and his brother, while their father worked in the watermelon farm about three miles away. Their aunts made sure that the boys were well fed and clothed, and taught them to do chores, like washing and drying dishes, caring for their own clothes, and yard work. However, they were harsh and punitive to both boys while their father was at work. The brothers were beaten frequently with a belt, and oftentimes had bruises, welts and swollen faces. Pete remembers the physical abuse that occurred almost on a daily basis. It became a ritual to be whipped with a belt or anything else that was nearby—such as a slipper, stick or paddle—that his aunts could get their hands on.

The boys had no refuge from abuse. If they visited with their mother, they were faced with physical and emotional abuse from either their mother, her boyfriend or her relatives. The boys struggled to see good in the people around them, but found nothing to encourage them to work toward building healthy relationships with their kin.

Pete and his brother felt the swiftness of their mother's boyfriend's back hand whenever they gave him the slightest look of discontent or unhappiness. Life was miserable for the boys and they vowed that they would run away as soon as they were able to. They had no refuge where they felt cared for—being loved was much more than they could ever expect from either parent.

Eventually, Pete's father became aware of all the physical abuse his sisters and ex-wife and her boyfriend were afflicting on his sons. He decided to change that. With the work at the watermelon farm coming to an end, he took his savings and bought passage to Honolulu on one of his friends' boats. It was the beginning of a new life for the boys. Their father, who had never left Moloka'i, was venturing into an uncertain life. He and his two sons would soon find out the harsh realities of city life without family support.

On O'ahu his father got a job picking pineapples, and they set up their home in a little shack behind a plantation house owned by one of his father's co-workers at the pineapple fields. It was the first time in their young lives that no one beat them up on a daily basis. The occasional spanking from their father seemed a far cry from the torture they had suffered in their earlier years.

Although they felt safer with their father, they still did not have his full attention. After backbreaking work picking pineapples, their father would come home exhausted and frustrated. He expected his sons to cook the meals and take care of the household chores. Oftentimes he just went directly to bed after dinner to get ready for his early morning job in the fields. Pete appreciated that his father was good enough to labor for them. But it was not the kind of life either Pete or his brother dreamed of for themselves.

Their plan to leave home was uppermost in their minds, and their desire grew stronger each day.

Since their father had no relatives on O'ahu to help care for the young boys during the summertime, he would drive them to the park in town and give them a loaf of bread and a jar of jelly for their breakfast and lunch. Pete remembered those days with fondness because he enjoyed the park where they met other kids and played games for the first time.

Struggling through the elementary and high school years, both boys became discouraged and disenchanted with education, and the life they were living with their father. Each day seemed like a year passing in their young lives. As soon as Pete's brother graduated, they both found jobs and rented a room in a boarding house. They both worked steadily, saving every penny for their airfare to the state of Washington, where some of their friends from O'ahu resided. There Pete and his brother made their homes and built many wonderful friendships. But on one gloomy day in a downpour of rain, Pete decided to return to Moloka'i. He missed his home island; wanted to return to the place of his birth.

Upon arrival, he learned of a new hotel being built, and applied for a job there. He got a job as the supervisor for the golf course, and began the task of setting up his life there. He found himself a bachelor pad in one of the local condominiums. Pete quickly became immersed in community activities, helping his longtime childhood friends on neighborhood projects and reestablishing himself in this place that he loved.

Soon his involvement as a volunteer in the high school's athletic program led him to Kiki, a young single mother with three young children between the ages of six months and three-and-a-half years old. Her young husband had been killed in an automobile accident eight months earlier and she was raising her family by herself. He had known Kiki in high school, and found her maturity and grown-up beauty appealing and mesmerizing.

They married soon, after a six-month courtship. She was his soul mate. She understood where he came from and what he wanted to attain in life. Soon they had two children of their own. Pete vowed that all five of their children would never have the hard life that he had experienced as a child. He was going to make sure that the children all knew how much he cared for them, and how much he loved them.

To show Kiki he loved her and his family, Pete treated her with respect and dignity, told her he loved her in front of their children, worked alongside her in the high school athletic program and community events, and was always there for her and the children.

As parents, both of them took great interest in their children's academic progress; went to their children's school for the occasional parents' events, showed pride in their children's accomplishments, and demonstrated how much they loved each other in front of the children. Pete and his wife used effective disciplinary strategies to teach their children about what behaviors they expected of them and avoided any kind of physical punishment.

After not seeing or hearing from his father for almost ten years, Pete was informed one day by one of his relatives that his father was dying of cancer and could not take care of himself any longer. Pete did not tell his wife because he did not want any contact with his father. The experiences with him had been too painful to repeat. However, when his wife learned of Pete's father's situation, she talked Pete into taking his father into their home. She insisted that Pete help his father through the tough times he was now experiencing. Kiki sent Pete to O'ahu to get his father.

The day he went to the Honolulu hospital where his father was, he said it was the strangest day of his life. He did not even recognize his own father. When his father walked into the waiting room where Pete waited anxiously, he recognized his father as the sad, elderly gentleman who he had passed in the corridor earlier that day.

When Pete went to collect the belongings at his father's residence, he found that his father still lived in a makeshift container and slept on a beer-box bed. Nothing changed, thought Pete. It was as if time had never even passed.

Although Pete took his father to their home reluctantly, Kiki welcomed him with open arms and was kind and caring to her father-in-law in his last days. Pete felt very good about his wife's kindness to his father. His own children got to know their grandfather, who had time to talk to them in a way Pete never saw him act with him or his brother. He got to see the better side of his dad. Within a year, his dad died. Pete was comforted knowing that he'd had the chance to care for his dad, and had been given the time to get to know his father better as a person.

As Pete reflected on his life, he shared that the one precious gift that every father can give to his children is to share himself with them. No other gift can be more valuable. To be there for them, to help them to envision the best for themselves, and to tell them that they are loved are immeasurable presents that any father can give his children.

Today Pete says that his life is full. Kiki, his wife of nearly thirty years, is the sun and the moon in his life. His children are married and have children of their own. He and Kiki make frequent trips to Oʻahu to visit their grandchildren. Pete says that he has enjoyed and attained everything he wanted in life. His wife and family make him a happy man.

At every stage of your life, you will learn some lessons. Depending on the lessons you learn, you alter your life so that it will be manageable and satisfying for you. Here are a few lessons from children that I've come across:

- Never trust a dog to watch your food.

- When your dad is mad and asks you, "Do I look stupid?" don't answer him.

- Stay away from prunes.

- When your mom is mad at your dad, don't let her brush your hair.

- You can't hide a piece of broccoli in a glass of milk.

- If you want a kitten, start out by asking for a horse.

- Never try to baptize a cat.

- Felt markers are not good to use as lipstick.

~~~

# Grains of Sand

(A Dozen Quotes)

~~~

We all have only one life,
but there are many ways of living it.

~~~

People treat you the way you trained them to
treat you. If you are being mistreated, you are
cooperating with the treatment;
so, if you do not like the way people are
treating you, just change the training.

~~~

When relating to people, a good rule
of thumb is to never make assumptions.
Ask questions to get a clear picture of what
they are thinking, or why they
are doing something.

~~~

~~~

Relationships are challenging
because there are people who
remember everything,
and then there are those who are
good at forgetting everything.

~~~

Do not make people underachievers
by over expecting something from them
that they are not able to give.

~~~

Your greatest asset is to be able to
choose your attitude. A happy person
is not a person with a set of
circumstances, but rather a
person with a certain mindset.

~~~

~≈≈

You cannot deal with change
if you don't change first.
You must do the thing you
think you cannot do.

~≈≈

It is when you give of yourself that
you truly give to others.

~≈≈

Help others whenever you can.

~≈≈

It is not fair to ask of others
what you are not willing to do yourself.

~≈≈

≈≈≈

Growth is the only evidence of life.
Growing old is mandatory,
growing up is optional.

≈≈≈

You are only effective if you are yourself.
If you are not comfortable with that,
then you are in the wrong place.

≈≈≈

reate better ways and new things by thinking and acting differently. You bring "spirit" to places, things and people when you bring the best of yourself—and then act in sync with them.

The serenity you create in your world will comfort yourself and others. It is when you are calm and peaceful that others will seek solace through you.

Your role in life may require the use of many skills, but your skill in dealing with people is the most important one. Relationships must be established and nurtured by you in order for you to reap their benefits. You make a real difference in any relationship. You can't be neutral in a relationship. You are either contributing to it or you are contaminating it. Remember that every relationship that you build or destroy is always your own.

Make happy memories to reflect upon when you need them. From time to time, even when you are feeling wonderful, flash back to the happiest moments of your life—they can nourish you because you know it is always possible to be happy. Some people can retain the pictures in their minds for years—they seem to recall these vivid moments in a second—while others act as if their mind's film has run out. They can no longer take pictures of happy moments—because in their minds there are no moments like that. A memory can be locked away in the mind's storage for whatever reasons, so that access to the memory seems sealed forever. But, just when you think you will never smile again, life comes back. You bring life back to yourself—it does not come from anywhere else. You have the incredible power to ignite a spark with the potential of flaming a great fire inside of you.

I remember a woman coming over to share a little story about Sophia Loren. She said that years back, Sophia Loren made a visit to New York. While there, she was robbed of her jewelry worth hundreds of thousands of dollars. During her visit, she was on the Merv Griffith talk show. On the air, Sophia was asked how she felt about the loss of her precious gems. Mr. Griffith made it a big thing—he said that she must be devastated over such an incident. Then he asked, "Don't you just want to cry over losing these precious gems?" Sophia looked him straight in the eye and said, "No. I don't cry for anything that doesn't cry for me." As far as Sophia was concerned, it was an unfortunate occurrence in her life, but not enough to bruise her self-esteem or strong belief in what counted most in life—people who cared for her.

# A Father's Estimation of His Daughters

Absalon Pascual was a father of five daughters—Sally, Catherine, Adeline "Deli," Merlyn and Eleanor. He was married to their mother, Maxine, his hometown sweetheart, for nearly fifty years. Born and raised in the Philippines, Absalon left home with his brother when both were in their twenties and headed for Chicago, where they both worked as waiters for three years in restaurants and hotels. They enjoyed what they did and were very good at it.

After a few years, Absalon and his brother returned to their homeland and opened a restaurant and catering business. He soon acquired the nickname "Chicago" from the local residents because he had lived in that exciting city, and talked so much about it. It was at that time, in 1934, that he married Maxine. The three of them worked hard to make their business a success.

Then in 1941, with U.S. troops being stationed in the Philippines, the U.S. government contracted their catering business to deliver homemade ice cream to the bivouac for the military to enjoy with their dinner every night. Chicago loved doing this job because he felt he was contributing to the war effort in his own way. He continued to serve the military until bombing damaged his restaurant. By this time, Chicago and Maxine had five daughters. Soon after the war, there was a call for field workers to work in the sugarcane fields of Hawai'i. Chicago saw this as a wonderful opportunity to help his family and get back to the United States.

In 1946, he left his wife and five daughters, and headed for Hawai'i. After his arrival in the Hawaiian Islands, he was assigned to the island of Kaua'i to work at the Lihu'e Plantation.

Within a few months, however, the personnel office at the company found out about Chicago's previous restaurant and catering experience, and transferred him to the plantation manager's household to work as a chauffeur, butler and waiter. Soon he became the manager's right-hand man, and had enough money saved to send $100 each month to his wife and daughters in the Philippines.

In 1954, with enough money for the fare on the President Lines' USS *Wilson*, Chicago sent for his entire family to join him on Kaua'i. They lived in back of the plantation manager's huge house in a comfortable three-bedroom home. Soon Maxine worked with her husband, serving as the cook and housekeeper.

With so many daily dining and household chores from sunrise to sunset, the girls joined their parents in making life comfortable for the manager and his family. They were all industrious. They labored seven days of the week. Even on school days, they would all go over to the main house to wash dishes, change the bedding and towels, and do whatever they could to help their parents, before they headed off to class. After school and on weekends, they also helped with maintenance of the lawn and the garden.

Even with their heavy work schedule, their father insisted that they invest time in their schoolwork. He told them that no matter what they did, they needed to do it well. Consequently, all five daughters became high achievers at their schools.

All during those busy years, Chicago found time to help his friends in need. If farmer friends needed to have their crops harvested, Chicago would be there working alongside them. When they were done, they would give him a variety of vegetables to take home for his family. Also, Chicago's fishermen friends would call him to help pick fish from the nets, and Chicago always made time for them. For his help, they would give him ten to twenty pounds of akule, a delicious fish, which Maxine deep-fried. That was the kind of person Chicago was to his family and friends.

The girls soon grew up and left their parents' home. The eldest daughter got married and the four other girls left for college on the mainland. Even after the

plantation manager retired, Chicago and his wife stayed on in the big house. Faithfully, Chicago and his wife took care of the household's every need until the plantation manager became bedridden and his wife too frail to take care of herself. Eventually, their son, who lived on O'ahu, relocated his parents to a nursing home on that island. It was an end to the era that they were most familiar with, and the Pascuals' future seemed bleak and uncertain.

About the same time, the plantation was offering all of its employees the opportunity to buy their own homes for the first time. The company employees had always lived in plantation-owned houses. Chicago and Maxine dreamed of a house of their own. But for the $13,000 house they wanted, they needed a down payment of $2,000. That was an enormous amount of money for Chicago, and he knew that he would not be able to raise it on his own.

When the girls heard of their parents' financial situation, they each contributed their savings to raise the money for the down payment. Yet when their father went to the bank with the $2,000 that they had struggled to put together, the bank manager told Chicago that the down payment was not enough to qualify him for the loan. The bank manager explained that because of Chicago's lack of credit history and the amount of his salary, he probably would not qualify for the loan. When Chicago wanted to add both his wife and daughters' salaries as part of the loan application, the manager refused to consider them as part of the loan approval formula.

Discouraged, but not defeated, Chicago went home. Sitting in the family room thinking how he could get that loan, he suddenly looked up and started taking down all five pictures of his daughters. Maxine, who was in the room with him, was puzzled and asked him, "Chicago, what are you doing with the girls' pictures?" Chicago looked at her confidently and said, "I've just thought of a way we can get our loan." "How?" Maxine queried. Chicago just winked at her and said, "You'll find out tomorrow."

With five framed photographs under his arm, Chicago walked into the bank and went straight to the bank manager's office. "Sir," he said, "do you have any children?" The bank manager answered, "Yes. I have a son." Then Chicago asked, "Does he go to college on the mainland?" "No," said the bank manager, "he goes to the Kaua'i Community College." "It is very expensive to send kids to college on the mainland, isn't it?" Chicago asked. "Yes. Of course," replied the bank manager, "that's why my son is at home attending the local junior college."

"Then let me show you something," Chicago began, "I have five daughters—four who went to college and one who is still in college. My eldest daughter attended college here in Hawai'i for two years before marrying. The four other girls went to college on the mainland. My second daughter graduated with a master's degree from the University of Washington and is working as a librarian. My third daughter attended Northwestern University and became a nurse. My fourth daughter got her teaching degree from Midland College in Nebraska, and my fifth daughter will be graduating with her teaching degree in June from Midland College. And," Chicago continued, "they all attended college with full scholarships."

Chicago concluded, "Despite the fact that I had all these girls in college, I have managed to be debt free throughout my life. I never believed in borrowing money because I always saved for what we needed, or found other honest means of getting what we wanted. However, now that I need to borrow for the house that I want for my family, do you think you can trust me for a $13,000 loan?"

The bank manager told Chicago, "This is the first time I ever had such a compelling presentation for a loan." With newfound confidence in Chicago, the bank manager gave him approval for the loan based on Chicago's incredible belief in his daughters and the way he had managed his life.

Happily, Chicago went home to tell Maxine and his daughters of their team effort in securing their dream house. They were ecstatic—all of their hard work and perseverance had paid off. None of his five daughters ever forgot that experience. Even now, when they set new goals for themselves, they can hear their father's voice reminding them, "There is no such thing as you can't do it…. You have to find a way to get something if it is truly valuable to you." To his family, Chicago left a legacy of hope that lives on in his children and grandchildren.

~≈≈

# Grains of Sand

(A Dozen Quotes)

~≈≈

Separateness is not natural.
It is in the human connection that we
become all that we can be.

~≈≈

You can have only two things in
life—reasons and results.
Reasons don't count.

~≈≈

Be in charge of the circumstances
in your life; options keep you
from feeling trapped.

~≈≈

~~~

You will not try new things if your fear of failure is greater than your joy of success.

~~~

Friendship should not be thought of as some-thing we get, it is something we give.

~~~

The nice thing about life is that the more we share, the more we have.

~~~

Results are the best proof of ability.

~~~

There is nothing so rare
as a favor done without a purpose.

~~~

≈≈≈

The best indicator of success is how much you
have grown in terms of being the best that you
possibly can be—and liking yourself in the
process.

≈≈≈

People are the problems and
solutions to every human endeavor.

≈≈≈

Let no one come to you
without leaving better.

≈≈≈

There are very few things that nurture
relationships as much as kindness—
pure and simple.

≈≈≈

**H**ave a broad perspective of life that encompasses everything in the universe. You will begin to realize the value of life and your role in it.

Happiness is something that comes and goes in waves. Trying to have it all the time will frustrate you. Accept what is in your life at the time, deal with it, learn from it, and find ways to feel good. This strategy is a faster track to happiness. Sometimes you have to let go of something that you tried hanging onto without satisfaction. You need to maintain a delicate balance between taking charge of your life and working with what comes your way.

A no-fail, feel-good strategy to feeling happy is good, old-fashioned giving. When you give, you feel more connected to other people. You never truly do anything for other peoples' benefit—you do it because it makes you feel good. Be generous and grateful at the same time. Helping to brighten other people's lives is a matter of giving, and knowing how to receive in a gracious and grateful way.

It occurs to me that while it is easy to give to others, and to feel the satisfaction of making them feel better, it is not quite so simple to receive another person's gift, or help in a manner that makes them feel good as well. If you're anything like me, you'll say something like, "You didn't have to do that" or, "Why did you do that?" Surely, there must be a more appropriate response to gracious receiving. Perhaps the response, "Thank you for thinking of me, I do appreciate your thoughtfulness," would be a good start.

All of us need to be reminded that while we are doing things for others, they in turn may feel so grateful that sometimes they want to reciprocate. When people thank you for doing such wonderful things for them, help to make them feel good about doing things for you as well. One of the most effective strategies that I know of is to tell the person, "You are so kind, thank you." Everyone wants to be considered kind. It is the most powerful and influential quality that touches another person. Once you touch a person's heart, you leave a lasting imprint no one else can erase.

Help to make someone else's life easier—it'll make you feel good. Why should anyone struggle when you know that you can help? All human beings experience suffering to some degree in their lives. You must be ready to face suffering, knowing how to change and shift your perspective so that you can manage difficult situations that may arise. Pain and change—even during good times—are part of life and need to be addressed. How you view your struggles can make it easier for you to go through the change experience.

Ask yourself some questions, like: Did I contribute to this? Is it making me stronger? What have I learned from this painful experience? What will I do differently next time? The answers to these questions will help you to learn something from the experience.

Whether you like it or not, you are enrolled in a full-time informal school called Life. You will have many opportunities to learn things that will enrich and fill your life with happiness. You will also find some of the lessons meaningless or irrelevant. Nevertheless, they will also teach you something about yourself that you didn't know before, so be open to the lessons of life.

Be aware of how fortunate you are—if you have good health, live where you love to be, have a wonderful, close relationship with someone, enjoy the job you go to every day—it will keep you from taking your happiness for granted and help you to appreciate it more.

You can be much happier with close, caring relationships in your life. You need to prioritize relationships so that you can pave a surer, smoother path to happiness, rather than chasing after wealth, status and power. Intimate relationships can bring security and serenity into your life. Closeness and warmth can be extended to friends and family—sometimes even to strangers, when you develop feelings of empathy rather than isolating yourself. Create a strong sense of connection by reminding yourself what you have in common with other people, instead of what separates you.

One of my most fun times came through two young men I met in my apartment building. I was on the third floor, where our exercise room is located, and as I waited for the elevator, a kind-looking, slender young man with a sweaty T-shirt came out of the room and waited next to me. I turned to him and remarked, "You must have had a good workout today." He smiled and said, "No. I should work out more with weights, but I just came in for a quick one today." Then we both got in the elevator without saying another word until we got to the twelfth floor, where a tall, brawny young man wearing a tank top entered the elevator. Instantly, I turned to the slender young man next to me and said, "I'll bet he doesn't go for quick ones." At that, he and I just laughed. Then I explained to the muscular man about the conversation that had taken place before he came into the elevator. He laughed as hard as we did, and told us that his body was something he took seriously and he worked out every day for hours. After the slender young man got off on the twenty-ninth floor, we continued to have a nice conversation. When he got off the elevator on the same floor as me, he told me that he was a professional football player visiting his parents; coincidentally, his parents were my next-door neighbors.

The following afternoon, I told the young man's father about the meeting and what a nice son he had. Meeting the two strangers and having a good laugh with both of them demonstrated to me that we can all enjoy each other and share a wonderful sense of humor that transcends our differences. Meeting people can be an unforgettable experience, or something not worth remembering—your perspective will determine your experience.

One of my close friends was dining with my husband and me when the subject of mortality came up. My friend mentioned how life seemed to be passing even faster as we got older. She commented on how important it was for us to look at everything we do, and savor the moment and the person(s) that we are with at the time. She reminded us that sometimes we focus on such minutiae—things that have no meaning in our lives—that we tend to forget to see the larger, more meaningful picture of what life is all about. The next day, she sent me the following story:

## The Sandpiper of Joy

She was six years old when I first met her on the beach near where I live. I drive to this beach, a distance of three or four miles, whenever the world begins to close in on me. She was building a sandcastle or something, and looked up, her eyes as blue as the sea.

"Hello," she said. I answered with a nod, not really in the mood to bother with a small child. "I'm building," she said. "I see that. What is it?" I asked, not caring. "Oh, I don't know, I just like the feel of the sand." That sounds good, I thought, and slipped off my shoes. A sandpiper glided by. "That's a joy," the child said. "It's what?" "It's a joy. My mama says sandpipers come to bring us joy." The bird glided down the beach.

"Good bye, joy," I muttered to myself, "hello, pain," and turned to walk on. I was depressed. My life seemed completely out of balance. "What's your name?" She wouldn't give up. "Robert," I answered, "I'm Robert Peterson." "Mine's Wendy....I'm six." "Hi, Wendy." She giggled. "You're funny," she said. In spite of my gloom, I laughed too and walked on. Her musical giggle followed me. "Come again, Mr. P," she called. "We'll have another happy day."

The days and weeks that followed belonged to others: a group of unruly Boy Scouts, PTA meetings, and an ailing mother. The sun was shining one morning as I took my hands out of the dishwater. "I need a sandpiper," I said to myself, gathering up my coat. The ever-changing balm of the seashore awaited me. The breeze was chilly, but I strode along, trying to recapture the serenity I needed. I had forgotten the child and was startled when she appeared.

"Hello, Mr. P," she said. "Do you want to play?" "What did you have in mind?" I asked, with a twinge of annoyance. "How about charades?" I added sarcastically. The tinkling laughter burst forth again. "I don't know what that is." "Then let's just walk." Looking at her, I noticed the delicate fairness of her face. "Where do you live?" I asked. "Over there." She pointed toward a row of summer cottages. Strange, I thought, in winter. "Where do you go to school?" "I don't go to school. Mommy says we're on vacation." She chattered little-girl talk as we strolled up the beach, but my mind was on other things. When I left for home, Wendy said it had been a happy day.

Feeling surprisingly better, I smiled at her and agreed. Three weeks later, I rushed to my beach in a state of near panic...I was in no mood to even greet Wendy. I thought I saw her mother on the porch and felt like demanding that she keep her child at home.

"Look, if you don't mind," I said crossly when Wendy caught up with me, "I'd rather be alone today." She seemed unusually pale and out of breath. "Why?" she asked. I turned to her and shouted, "Because my mother died!" and thought, my God, why was I saying this to a little child?

"Oh," she said quietly, "then this is a bad day." "Yes," I said, "and yesterday, and the day before and oh, just go away!" "Did it hurt?" she inquired.

*75*

Did it hurt? I was exasperated with her, with myself. "When she died? Of course, it hurt!" I snapped, misunderstanding, wrapped up in myself. I strode off.

A month or so after that, when I next went to the beach, she wasn't there. Feeling guilty, ashamed and admitting to myself I missed her, I went up to the cottage after my walk and knocked on the door. "Hello," I said. "I'm Robert Peterson. I missed your little girl today and wondered where she was?"

"Oh yes, Mr. Peterson, please come in. Wendy spoke of you so much. I'm afraid I allowed her to bother you. If she was a nuisance, please accept my apologies." "Not at all—she's a delightful child," I said, suddenly realizing that I meant what I had just said.

"Wendy died last week, Mr. Peterson. She had leukemia. Maybe she didn't tell you." Struck dumb, I groped for a chair. I had to catch my breath. "She loved this beach, so when she asked to come, we couldn't say no. She seemed so much better here and had a lot of what she called happy days.

"But the last few weeks, she declined rapidly." Her voice faltered. "She left something for you...if only I can find it. Could you wait a moment while I look?" I nodded stupidly, my mind racing for something to say to this lovely woman. She handed me a smeared envelope, with "Mr. P" printed on it in bold childish letters. Inside was a drawing in bright crayon of a yellow beach, a blue sea and a brown bird. Underneath was carefully printed:

A SANDPIPER TO BRING YOU JOY.

Tears welled up in my eyes and a heart that had almost forgotten to love opened wide. I took Wendy's mother in my arms. "I'm so sorry. I'm so sorry. I'm so sorry," I muttered over and over, and we wept together.

The precious little picture is framed now and hangs in my study. Six words—one for each year of her life—that speak to me of harmony, courage and undemanding love. A gift from a child with sea-blue eyes and hair the color of sand—who taught me the gift of love.

Sometimes things happen for a reason. Never ignore or brush aside anyone as insignificant. You never know what that person can teach you. Everyone in life teaches, it is just a matter of how much you want to learn.

Position yourself for success every time with everyone. Make sure that where you are, what you are trained to do, and the people you select in your life are all vital elements in your plan for the life you want so that you can make it happen. A little chance or luck always helps, but do not put your life on hold waiting for it. Always position yourself to be in the right place at the right time with the right people. That placement will bring you harmony, good health, better relationships and increased prosperity.

There are things you might lose that you really do not want to lose; then there are things you might want to release to make yourself a better person. Sometimes you learn that both lessons can be combined into an important one, and can give you a deeper insight into your own life. Michael Donohoo's story about his football coach illustrates this well:

After his coach, Mr. Lionel Martin, died, Michael went to the beach to hear the soothing rhythm of the waves while thinking of this man who'd had such faith in him. He wore the championship jacket his team had won at the high school state finals. They had been victorious, and they all knew that it was their coach who had inspired them to greatness—not because he was an exceptional coach, but rather because he chose to be an ordinary guy with an extraordinary belief in the young people from a small high school near an ocean-front community. Mr. Martin made each player on the team feel that he was important for who he was, and recognized the gifts that each of them had to share with the others. He always told them that they had the power to transform their lives for the better.

Mr. Martin was always there to show the team simple ways of doing just that—like keeping his word, being a good listener, supporting the team members, thinking well of others, and helping when they needed his help.

It demonstrated to them that what Mr. Martin said was what he actually would do. It was easy to figure out the kind of person he was.

As Michael sat there, he could hear Mr. Martin's voice sharing these lessons tucked here and there into their practice sessions. As he sat pondering what this man had done for him, the rays of the mid-morning sun penetrated his polyester and cotton jacket, overwhelming him with heat. He removed the jacket, and placed it on the beach mat as he lay down for a nap. From deep slumber, Michael was awakened by white-foamed waves washing over him. Frantically, he ran to higher ground, forgetting the precious jacket and everything else on the lau hala mat.

For days Michael grieved over the loss of his precious jacket—the one that held so many positive memories of Mr. Martin and himself. He had been so proud to wear the jacket. Now he felt so lost without it. Michael waited on shore, thinking that if he waited long enough it would come washing up to the beach and back to him in the same shape as when it left him. He imagined that nothing would have changed.

However, days, weeks and months went without a sign of Michael's lost jacket. Then one day, while walking through a swap meet near the beach, Michael spotted his jacket hanging on a post at a vendor's booth. It was his jacket. He saw his initials, M. D., sewn in the inside lining. It was tattered and faded—its journey had been rough. Michael quickly bought his jacket and took it home with him. He sent it to the cleaners, but it never looked the same as before.

Yet as Michael examined it, he got the same feelings that he'd had before the jacket was lost. He had not forgotten what it meant to him. The memories flowed easily through his brain, like gentle waves gracefully dancing to shore. What was unforgettable to Michael was Mr. Martin's inspiration that encouraged him to do his best, to work hard for what he wanted, and the realization that he would be the most important player in his game of life. Michael never wore the jacket again, but it still hangs in his closet to remind him of its value in his life.

~≈~

# Grains of Sand

(A Dozen Quotes)

~≈~

They call the present a gift
because in it you can experience
the joy of today.

~≈~

We all get one life,
but there are many ways of living it.

~≈~

No one should retire from life at any age.

~≈~

There is always time to do
what is truly important. Do it.

~≈~

≈≈≈

The opportunity to excel is one
of the most valuable gifts
you can give another human being.

≈≈≈

Life is quite fair.
You have things that others do not have,
and others have things that you
do not have either.

≈≈≈

Your impact in life is not what you have
acquired, but what you leave behind in the
lives you have touched.

≈≈≈

Forget the past.
No one becomes successful in the past.

≈≈≈

≈≈≈

We never know who
or how much we influence.

≈≈≈

Keeping your word to yourself
and others establishes your worth in life.

≈≈≈

Make people feel special in your
company. Let them be who they are,
not what you expect them to be.

≈≈≈

No matter how bad things are,
no one can force you to
have a bad attitude.

≈≈≈